COLOR YOUR BLOSSO

FLOWER ADULTS COLORING BOOK

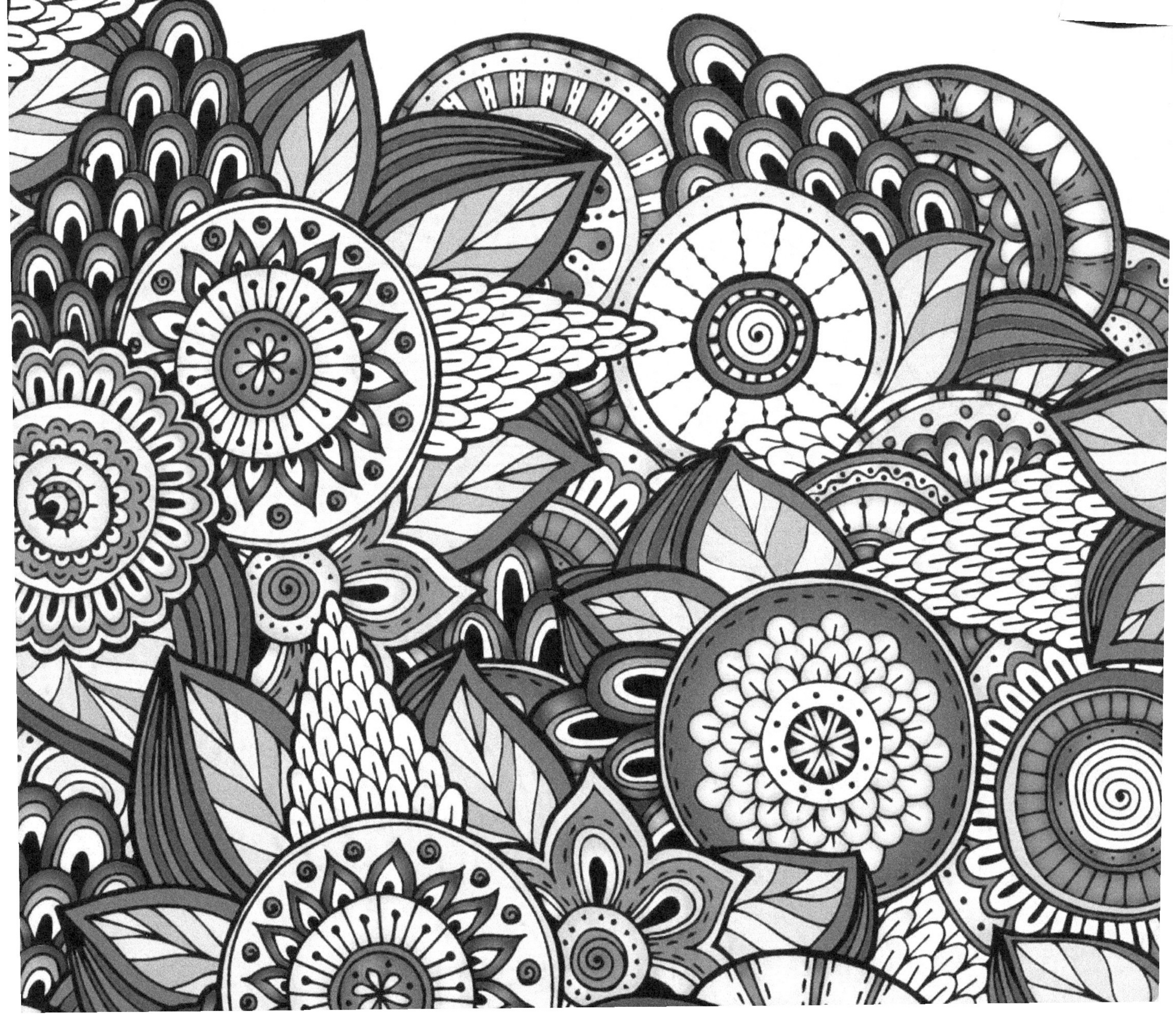

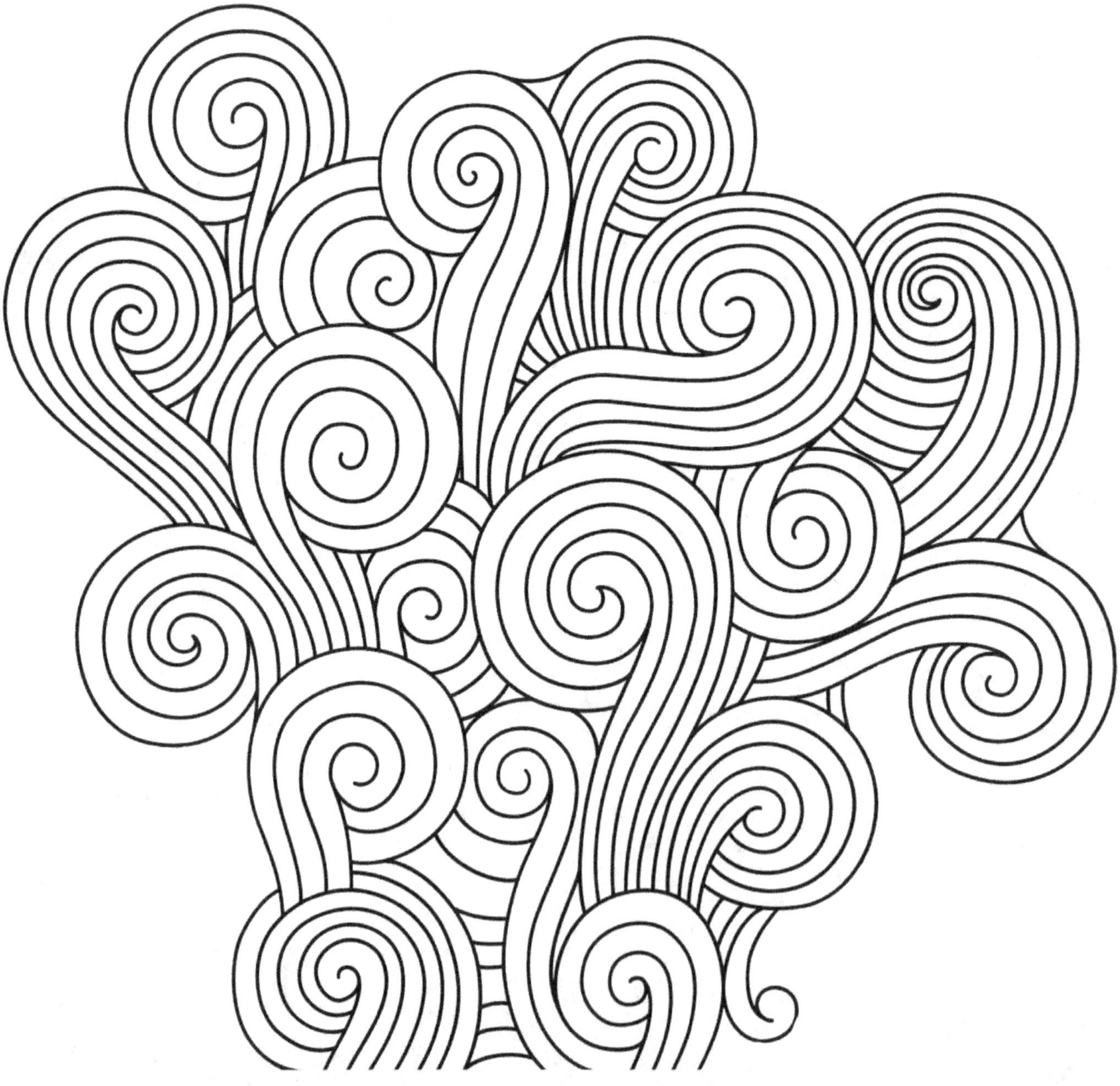

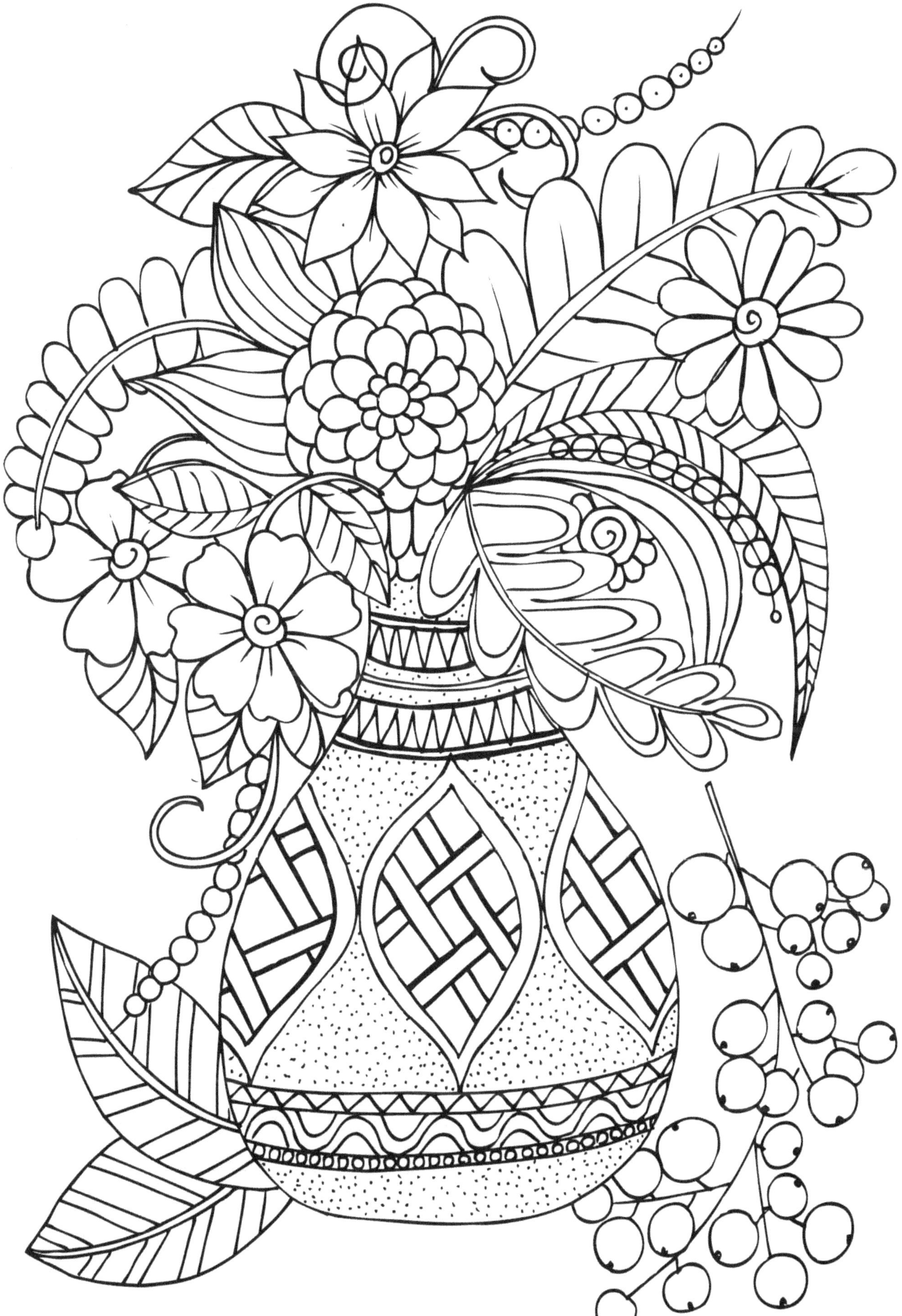

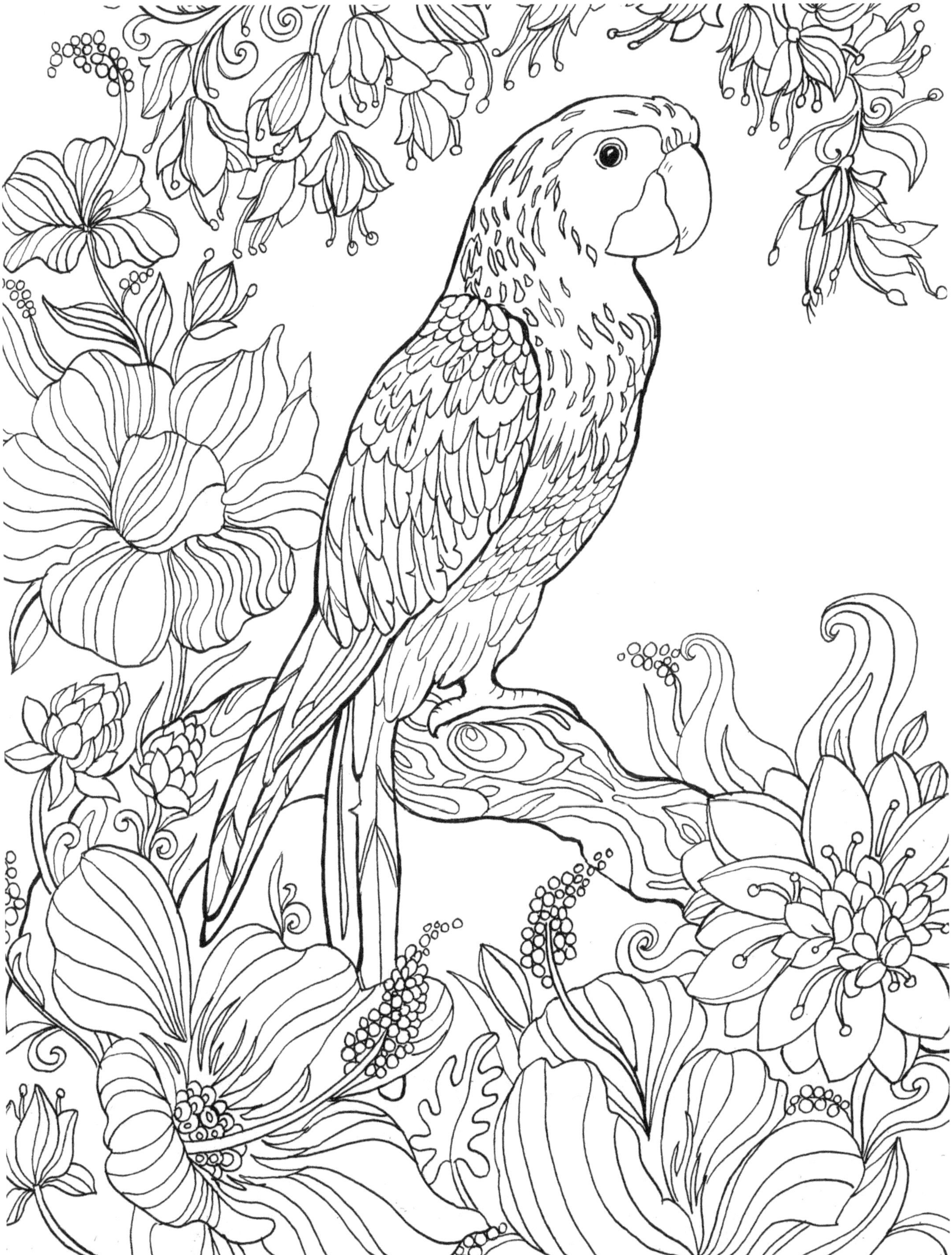

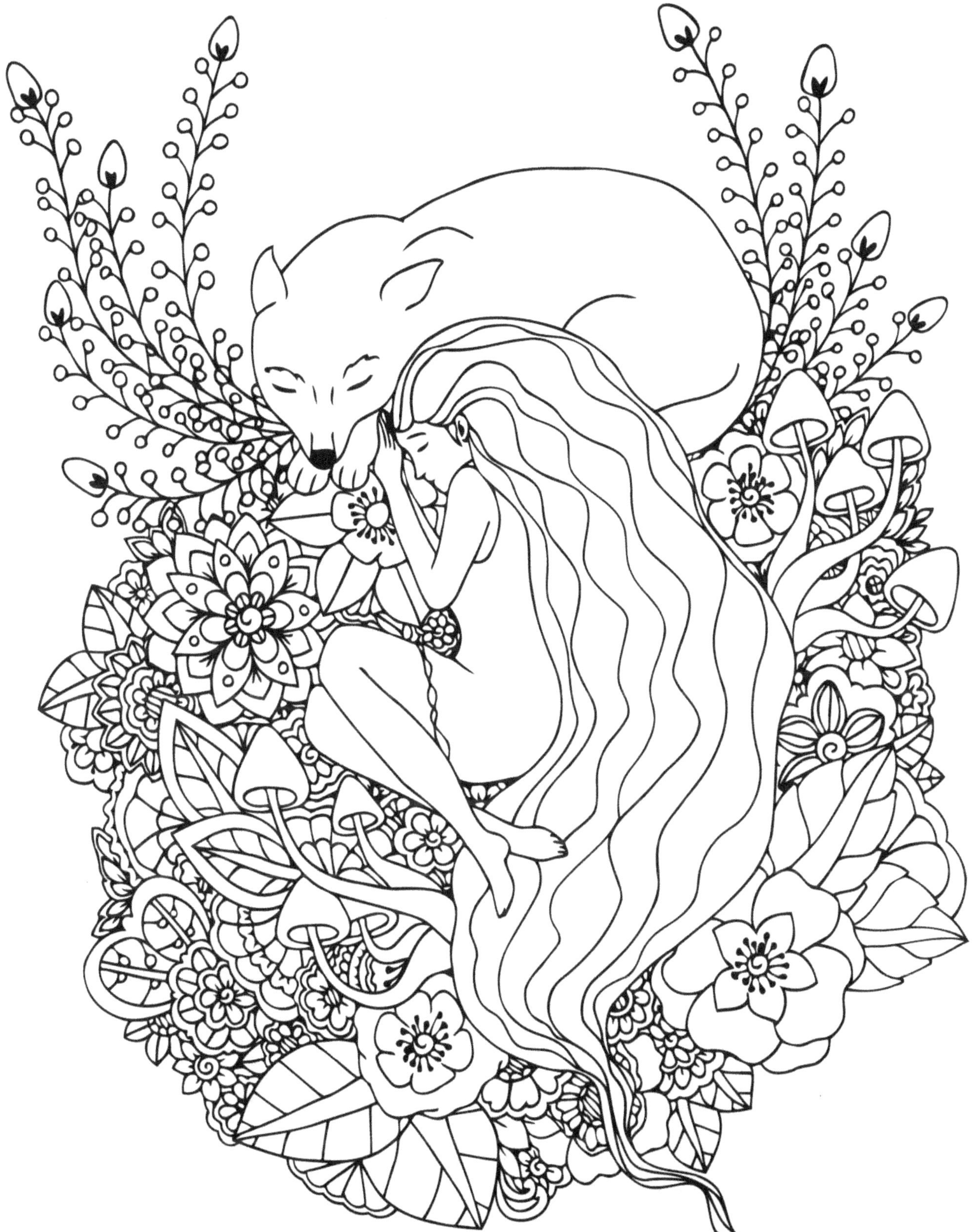

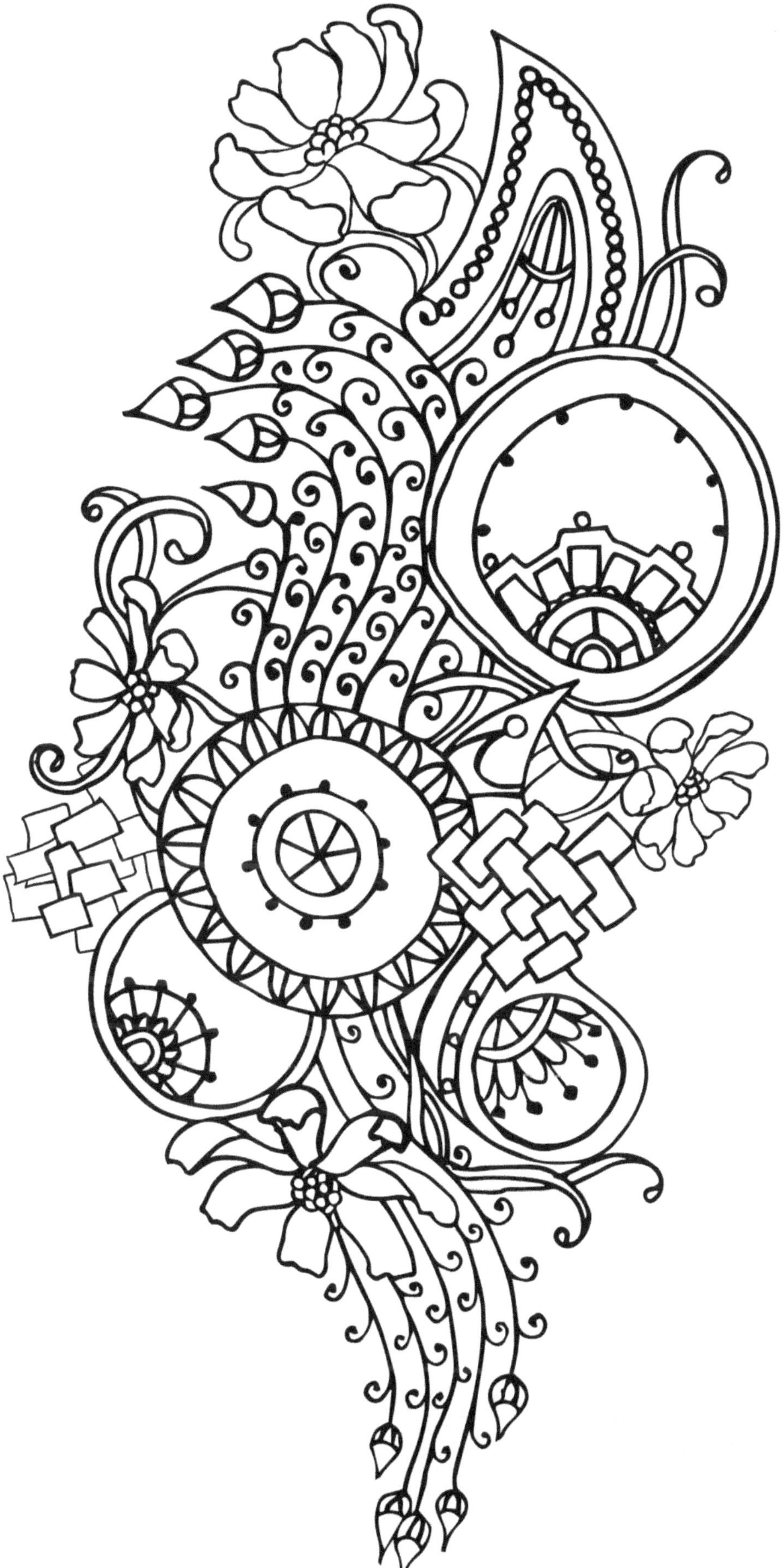

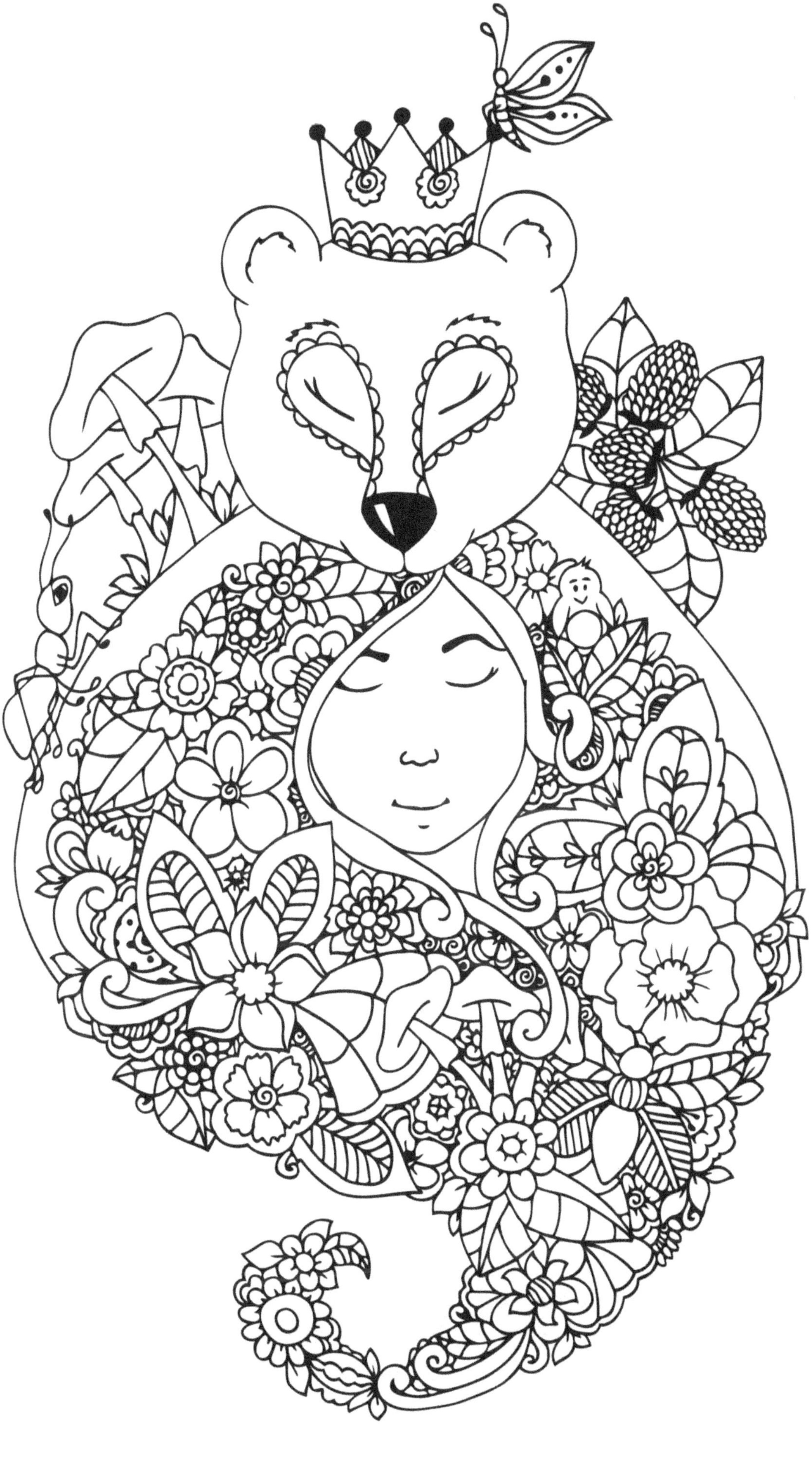

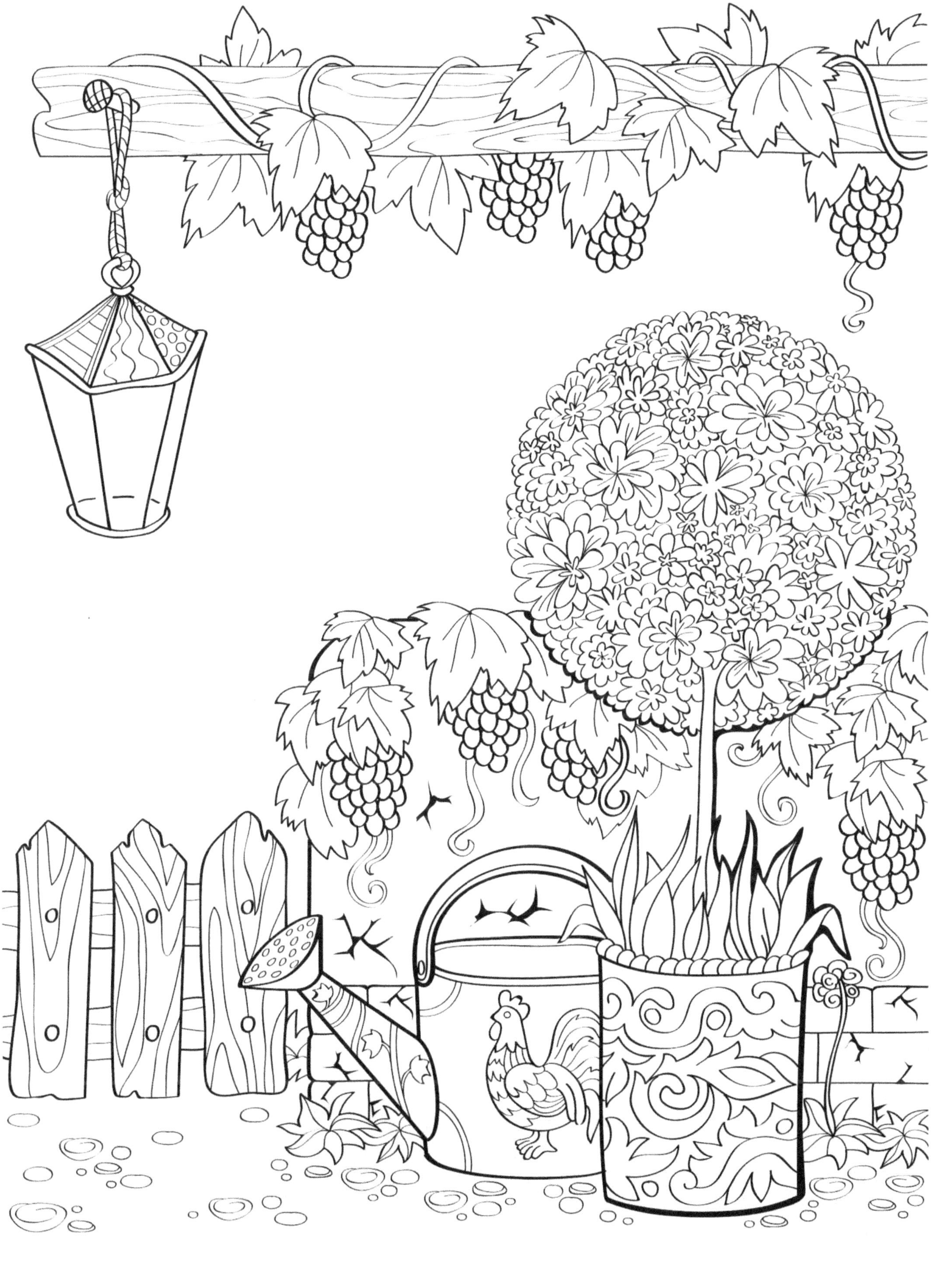

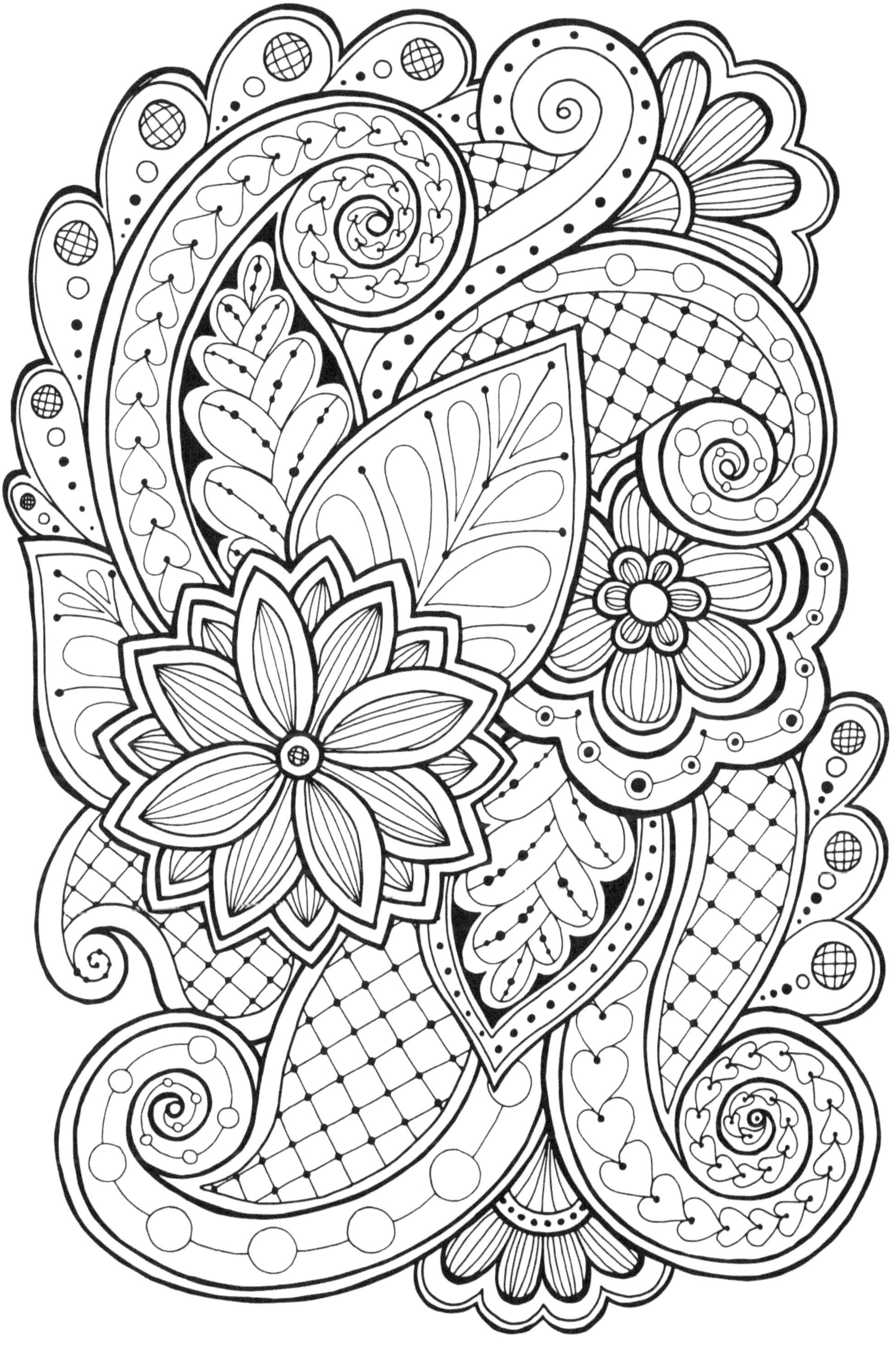

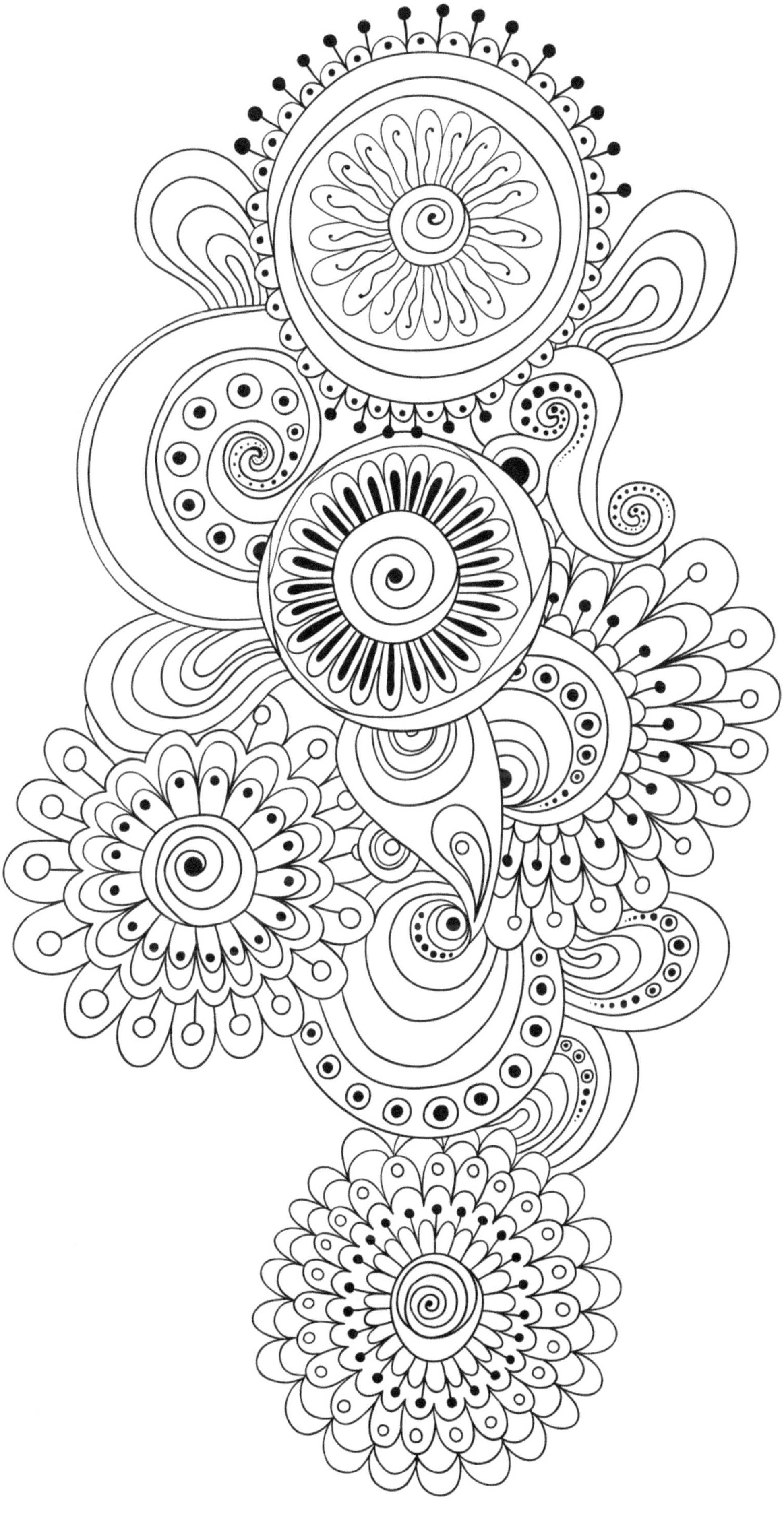

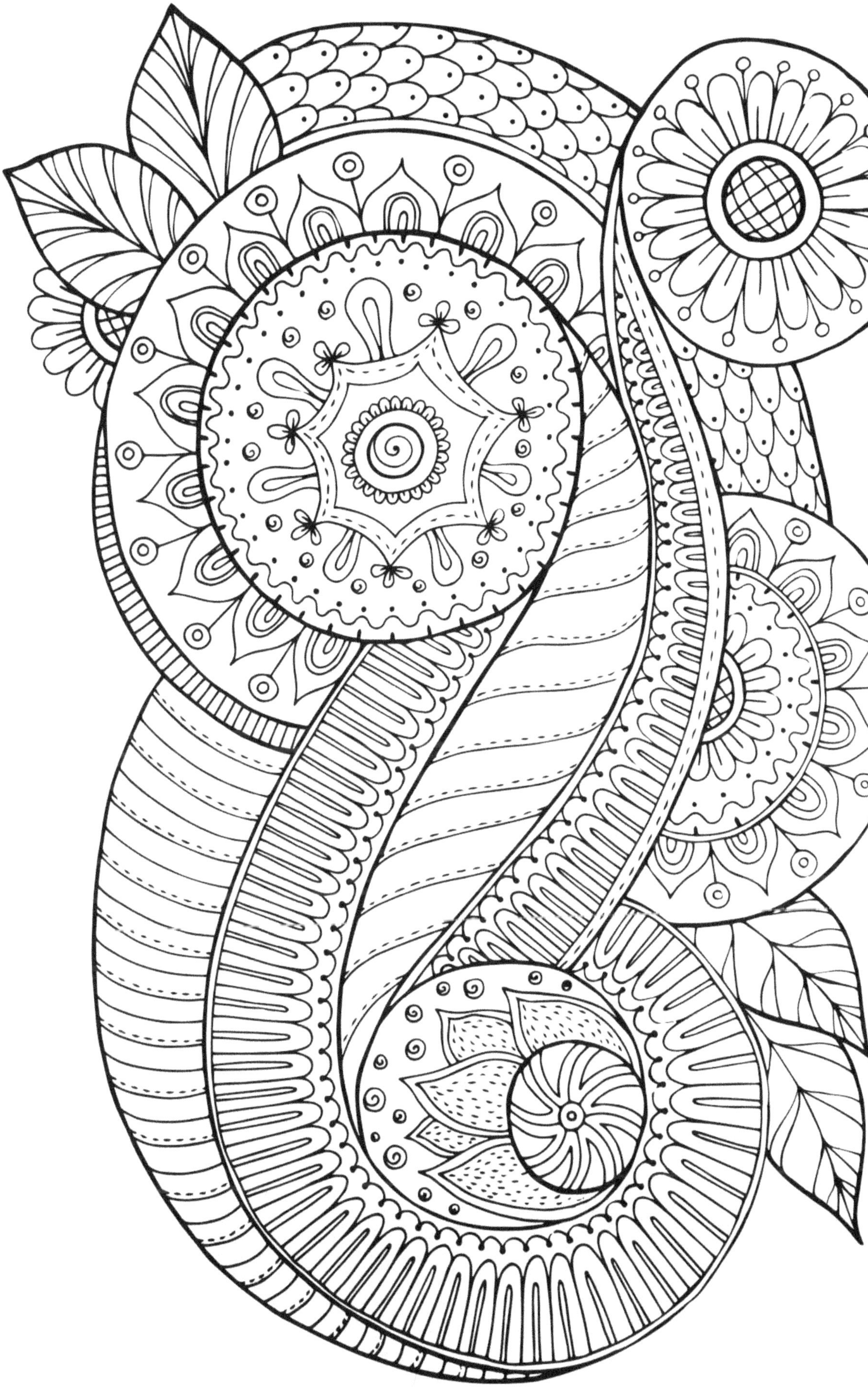

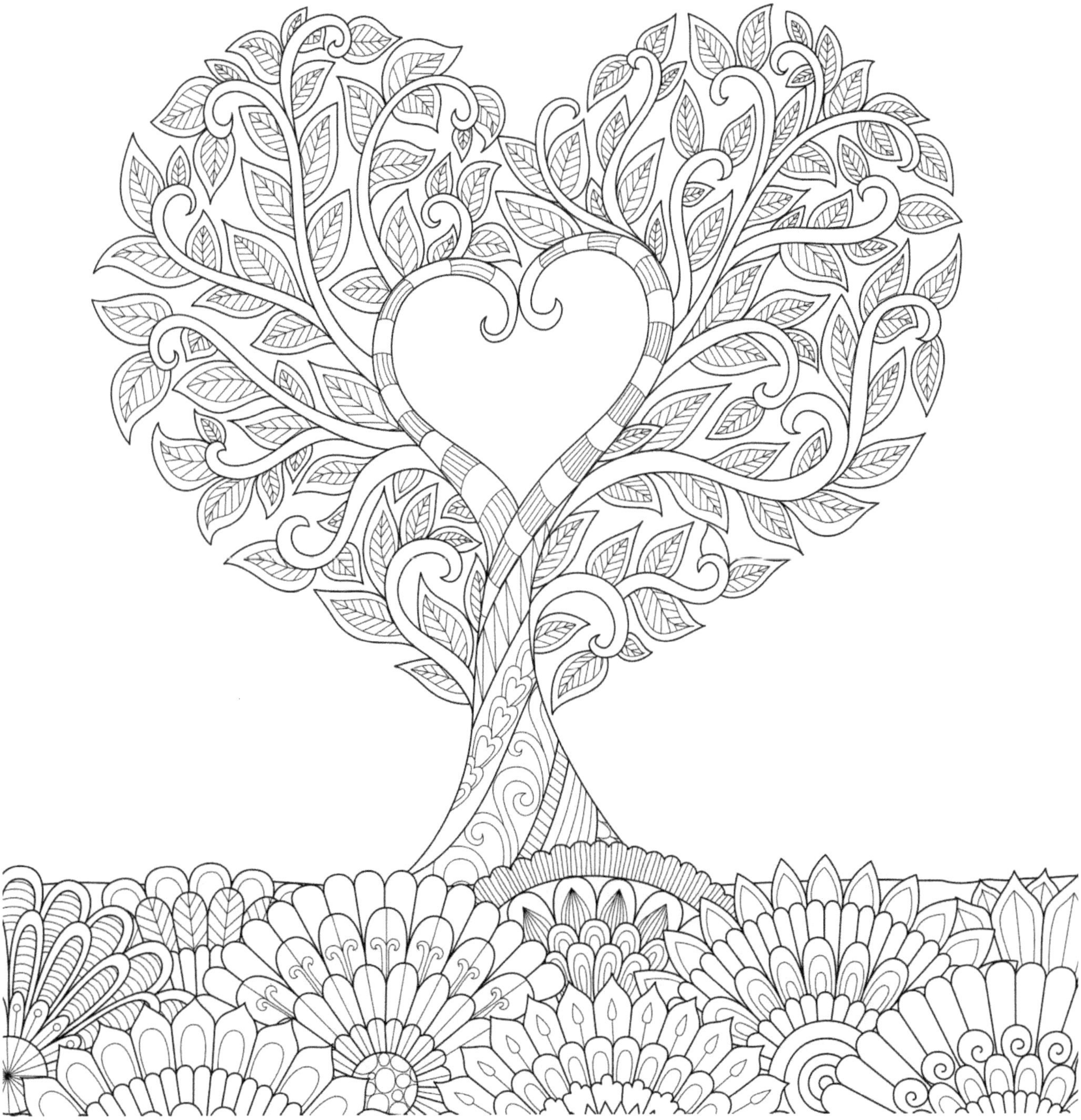

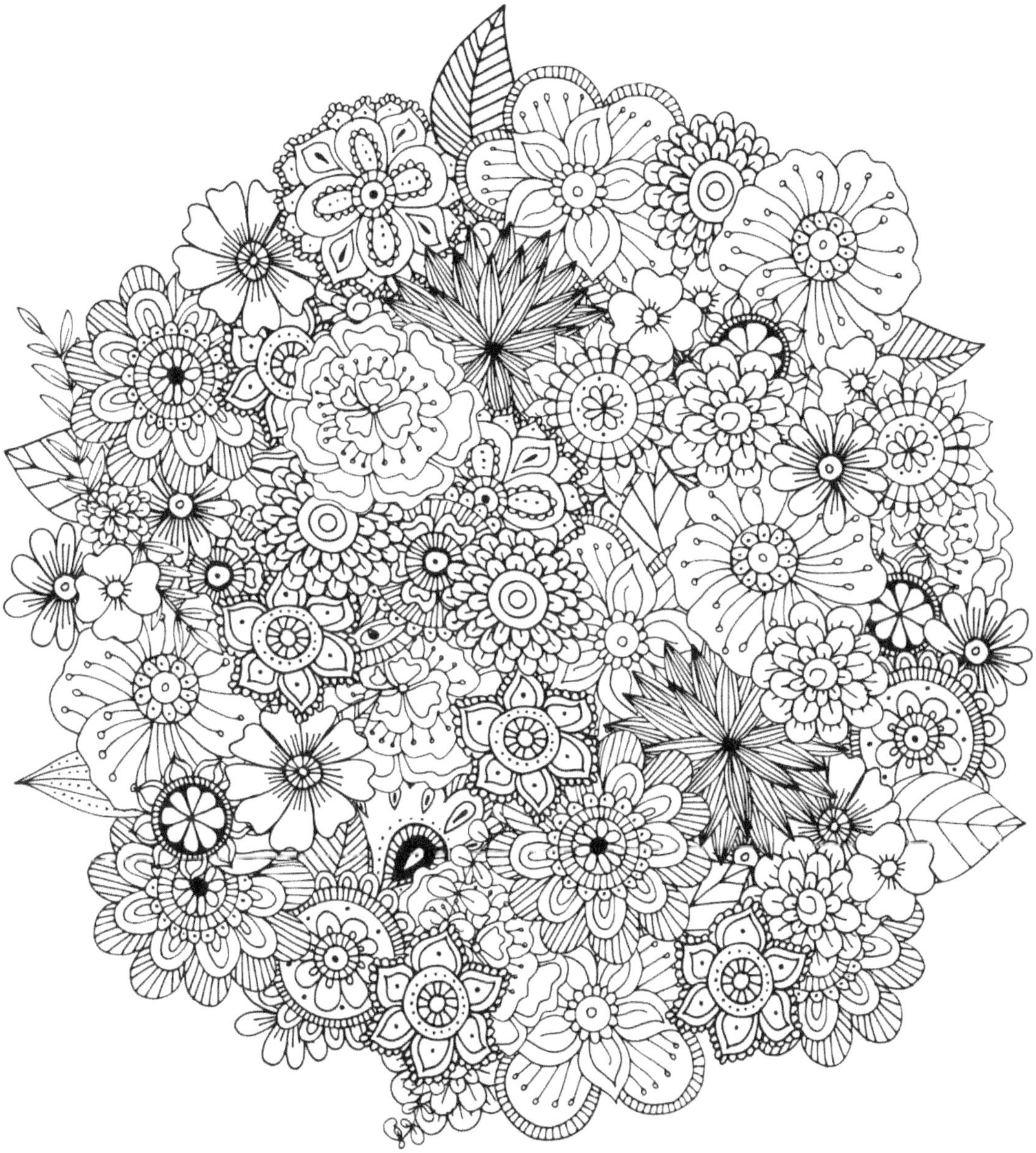

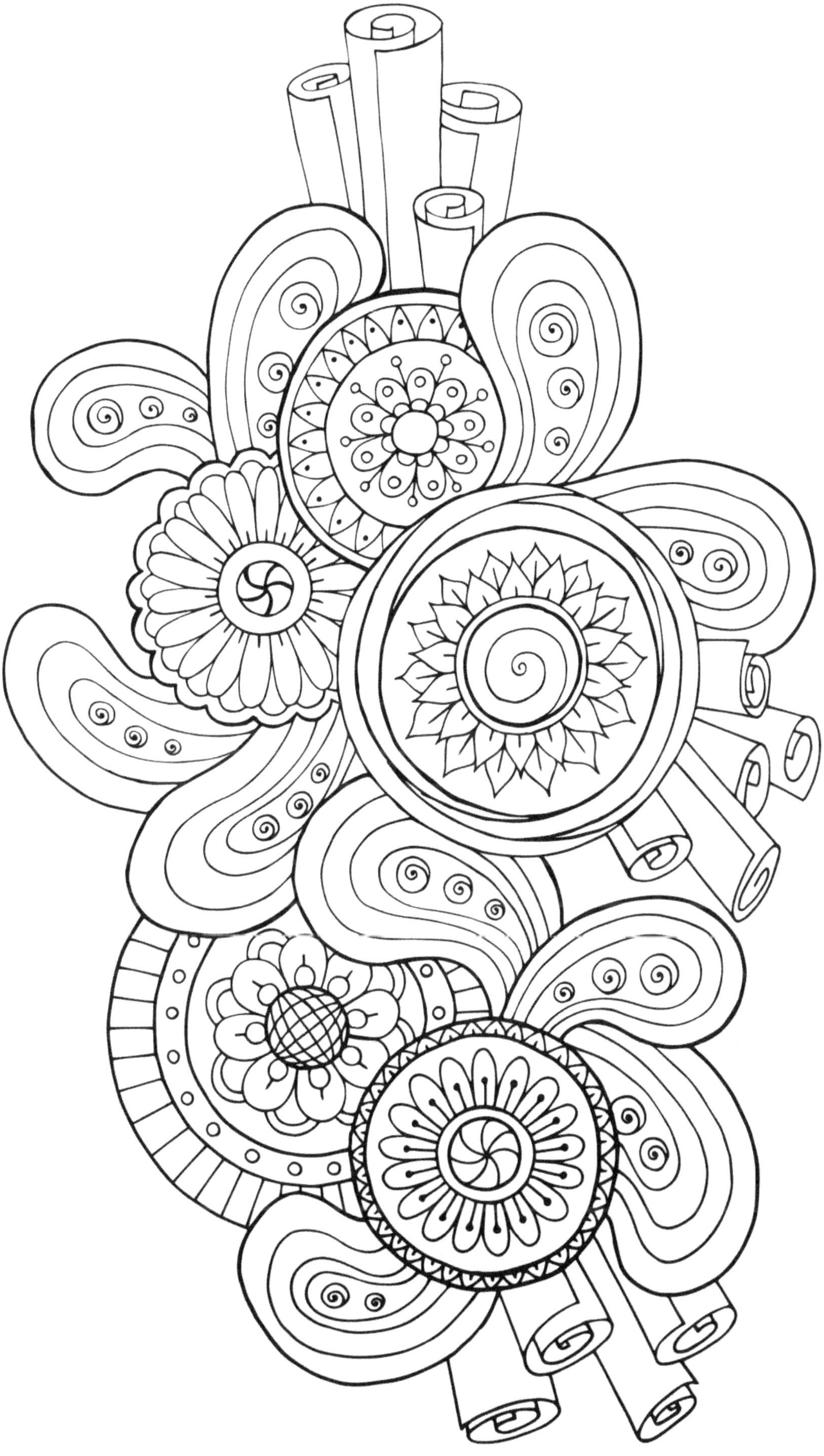

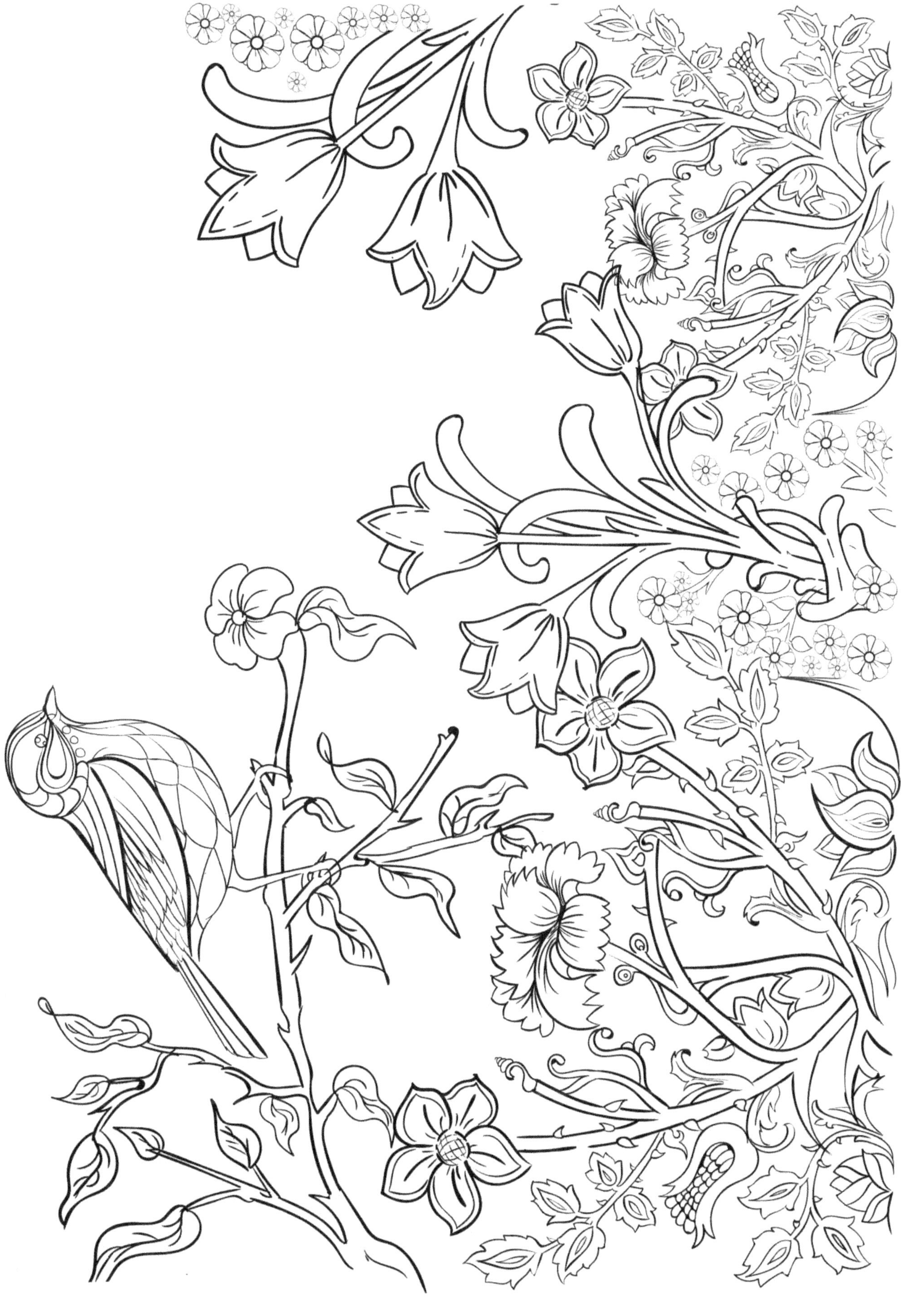

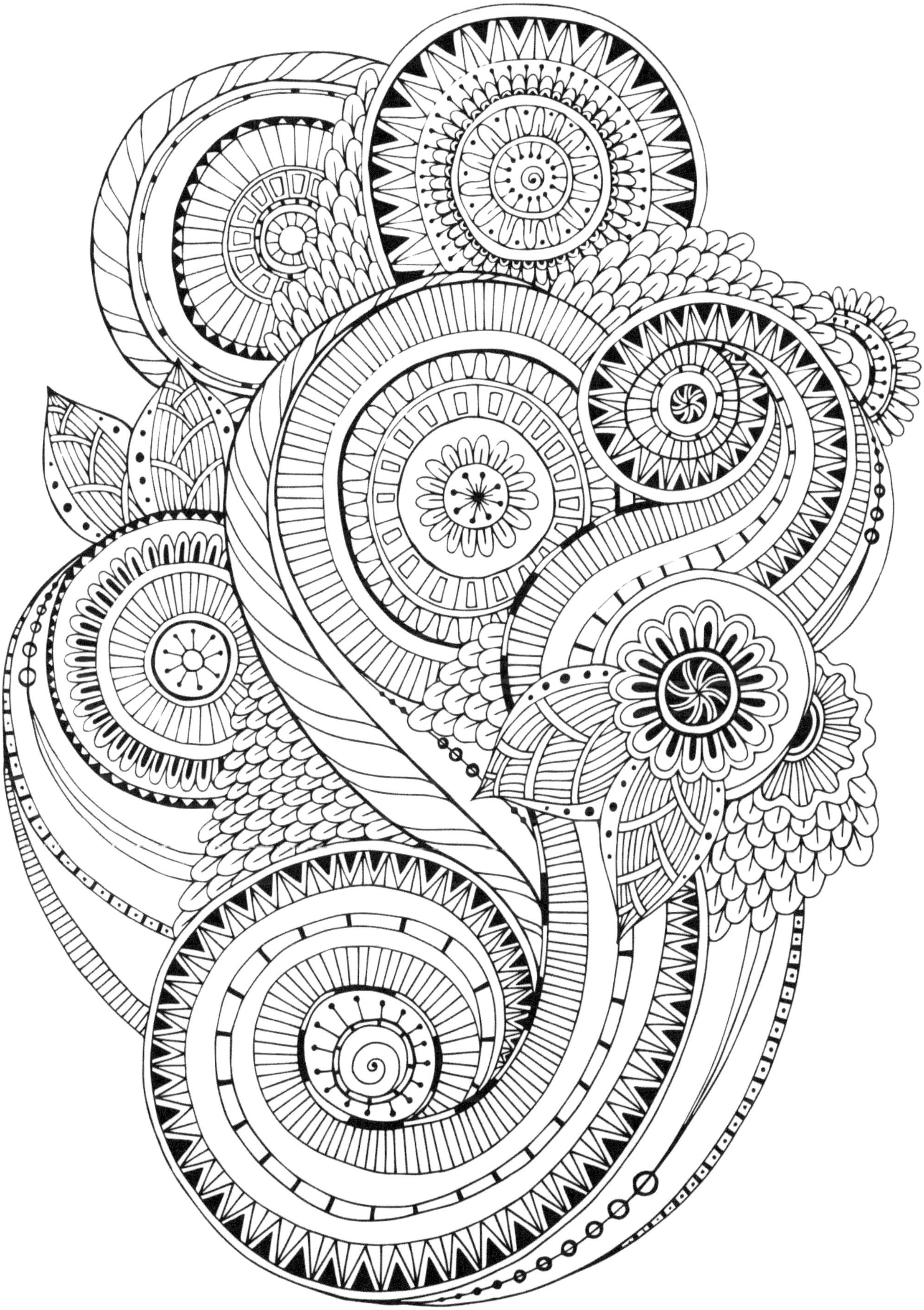

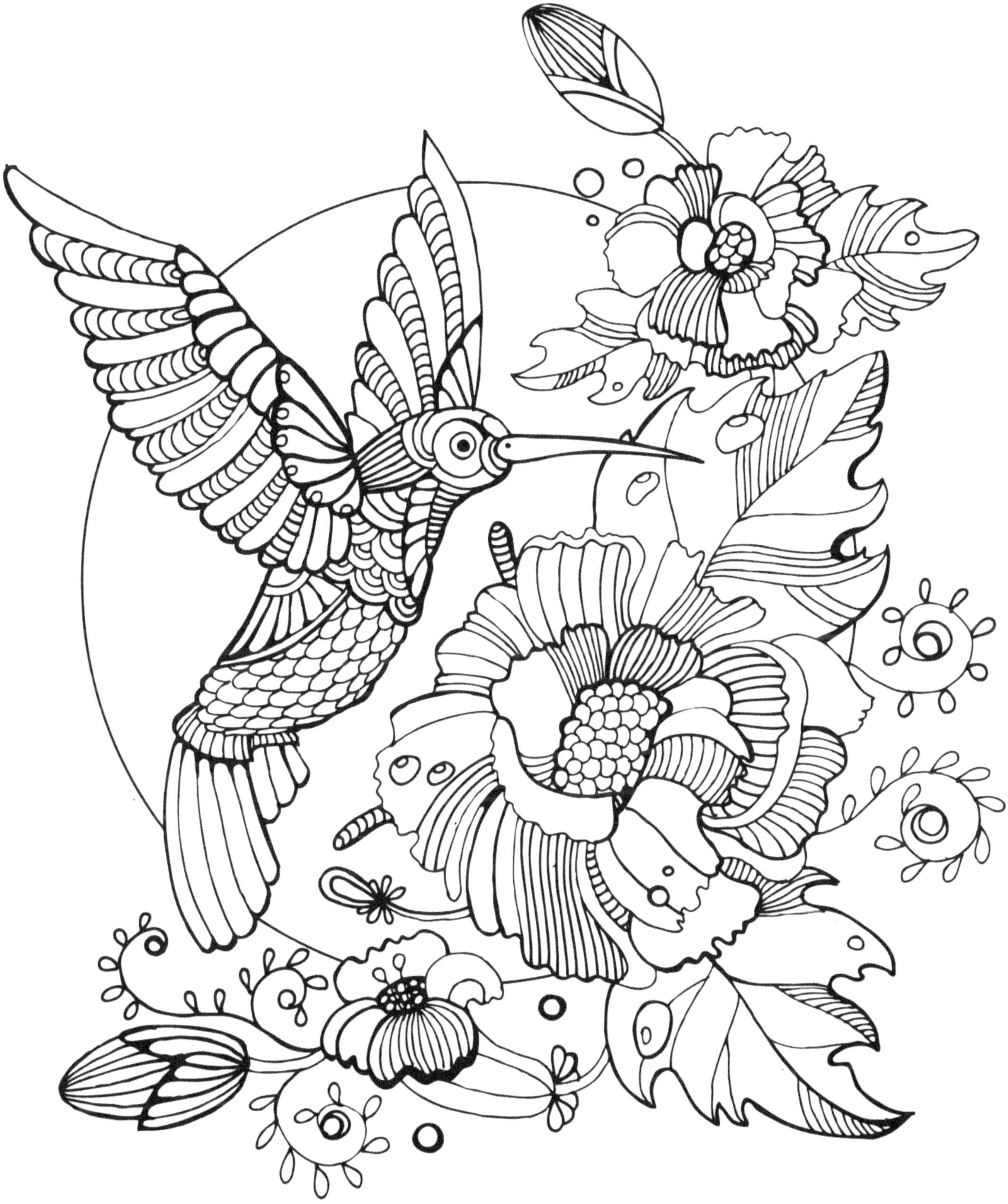

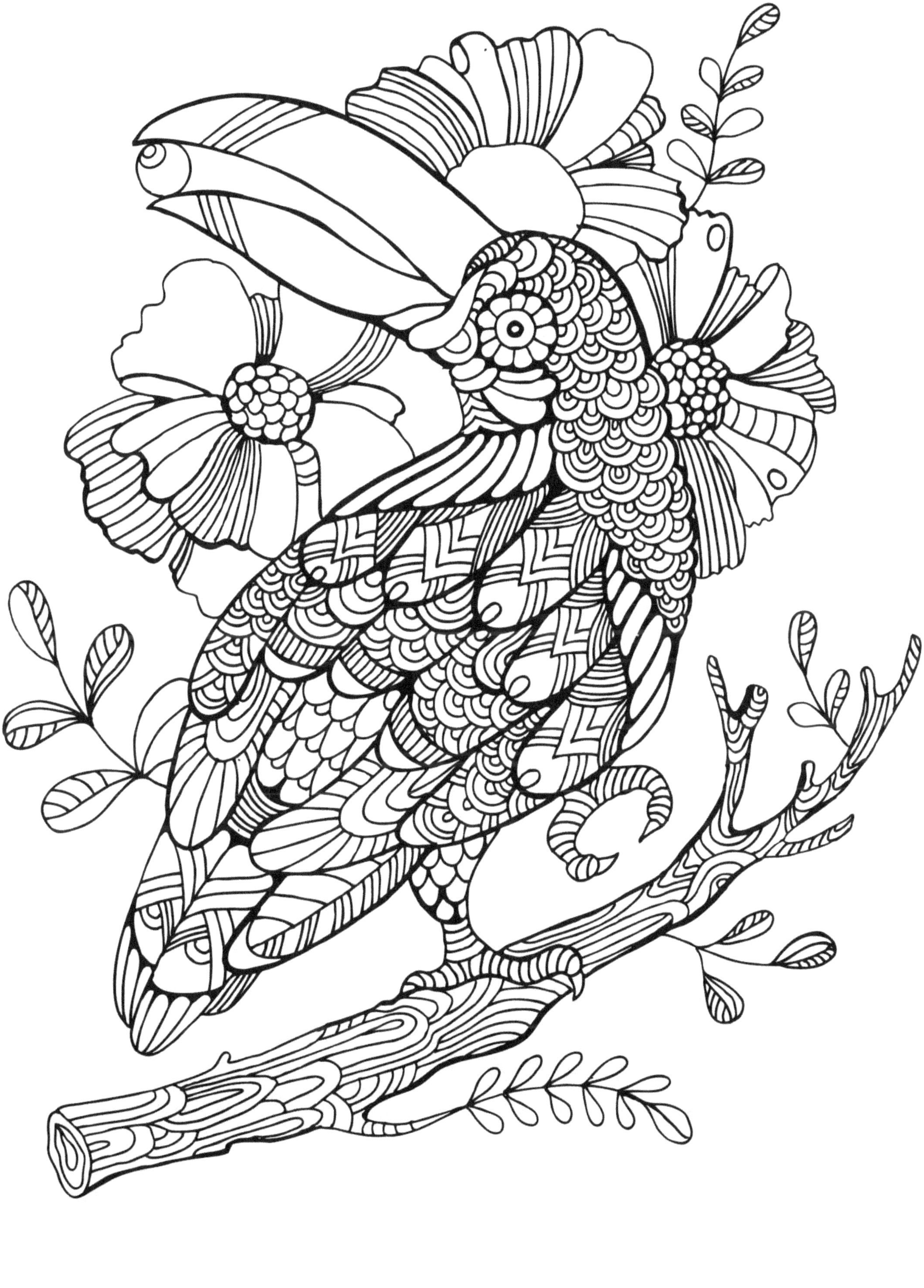

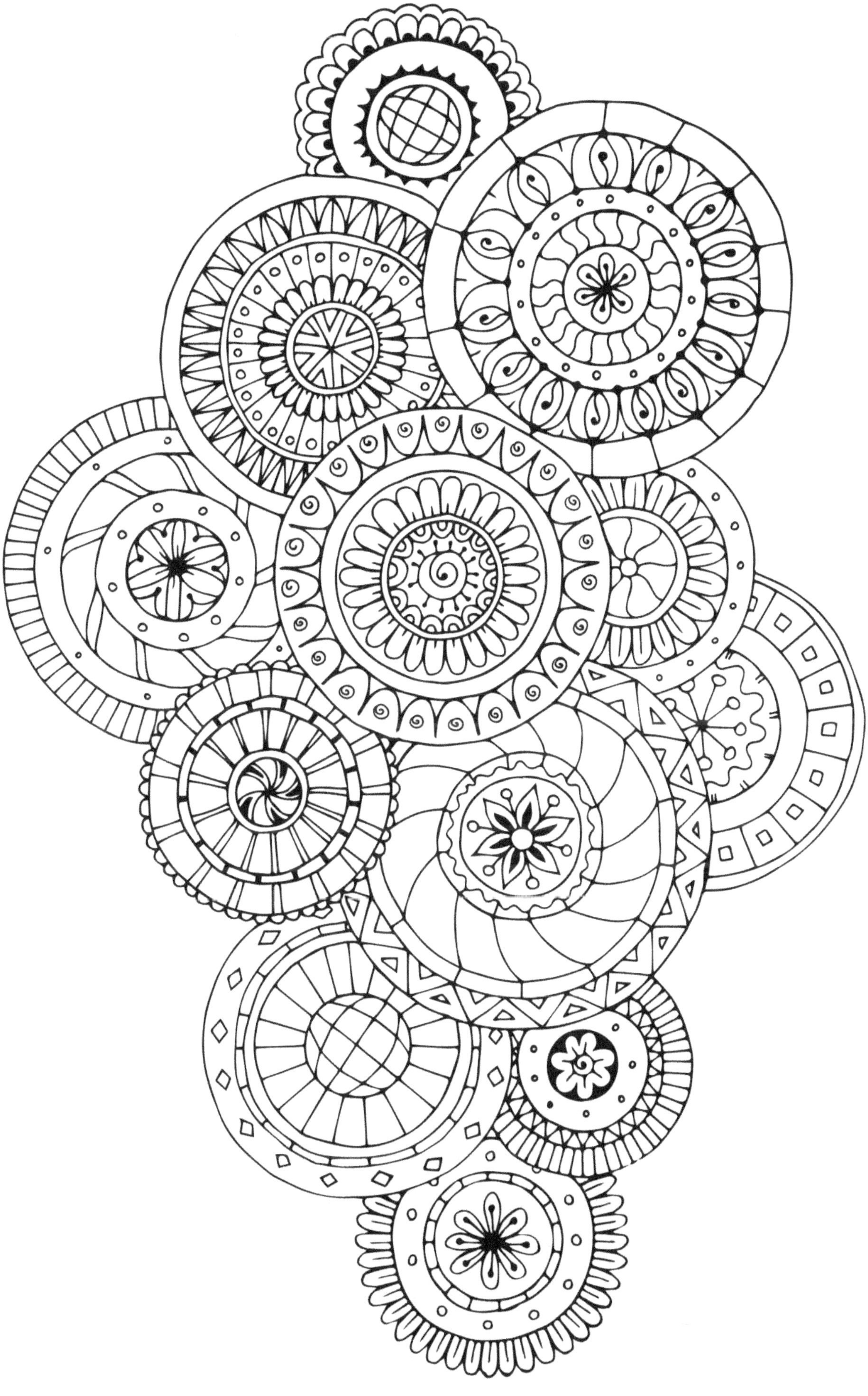

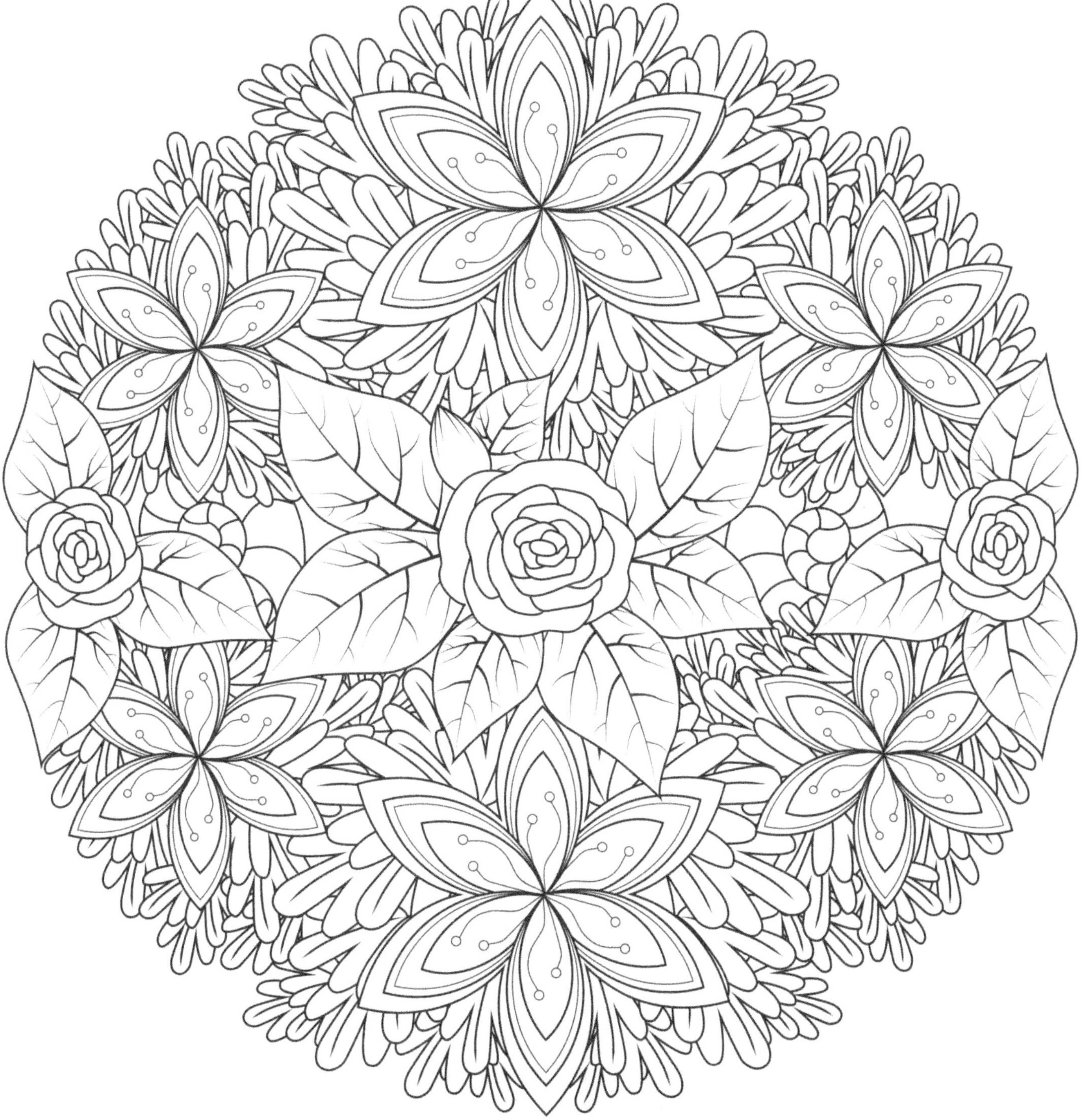

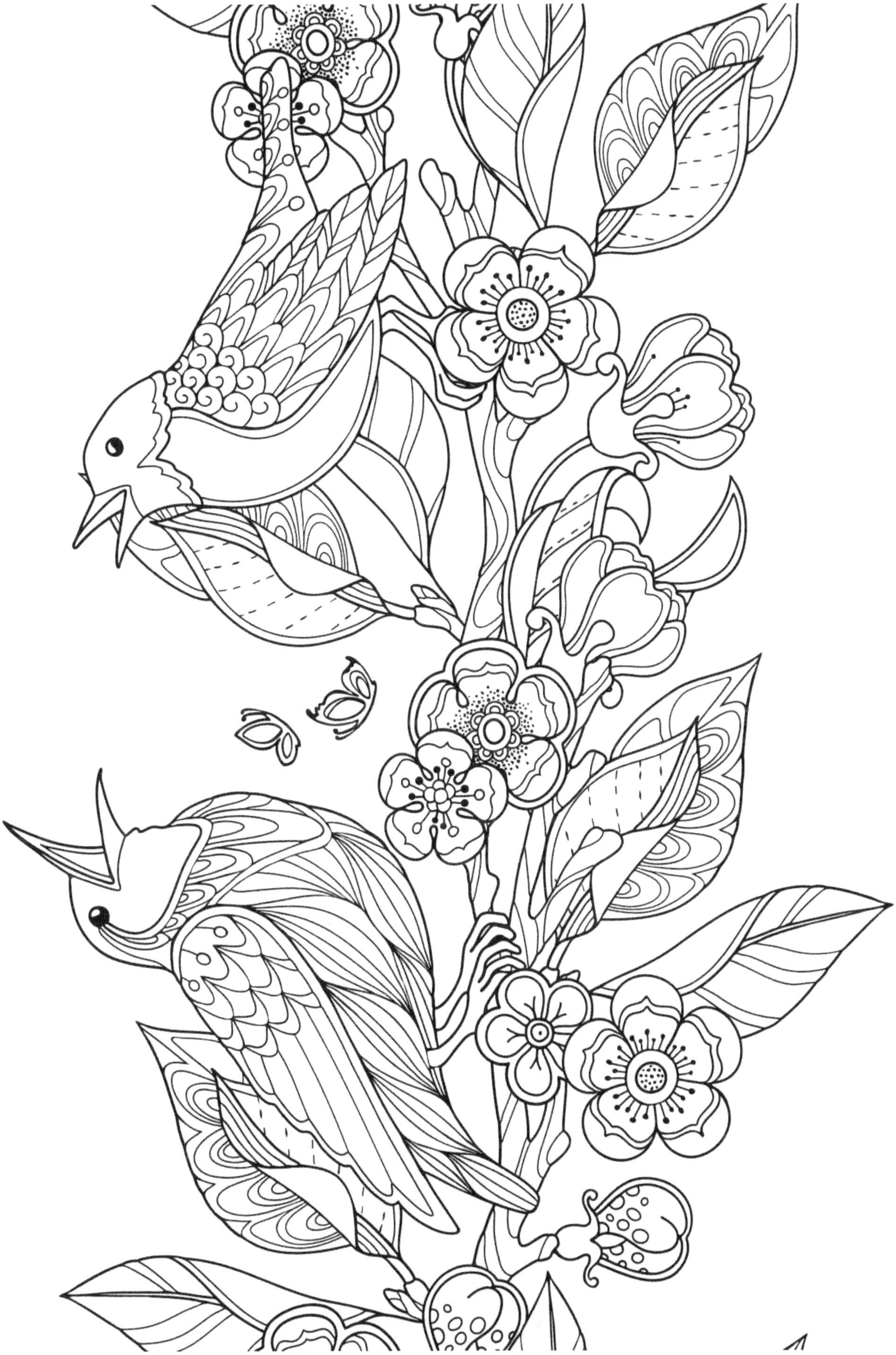

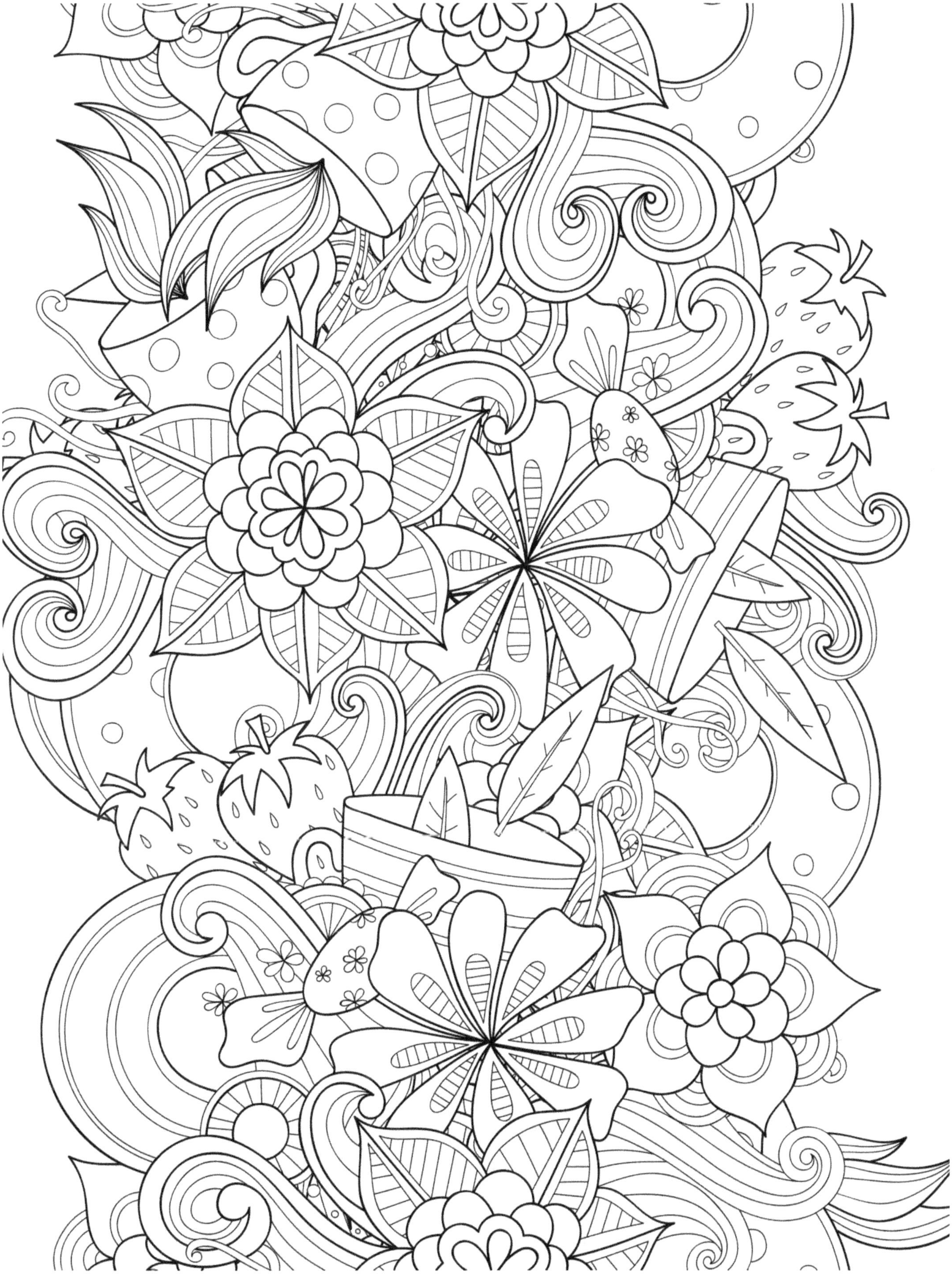

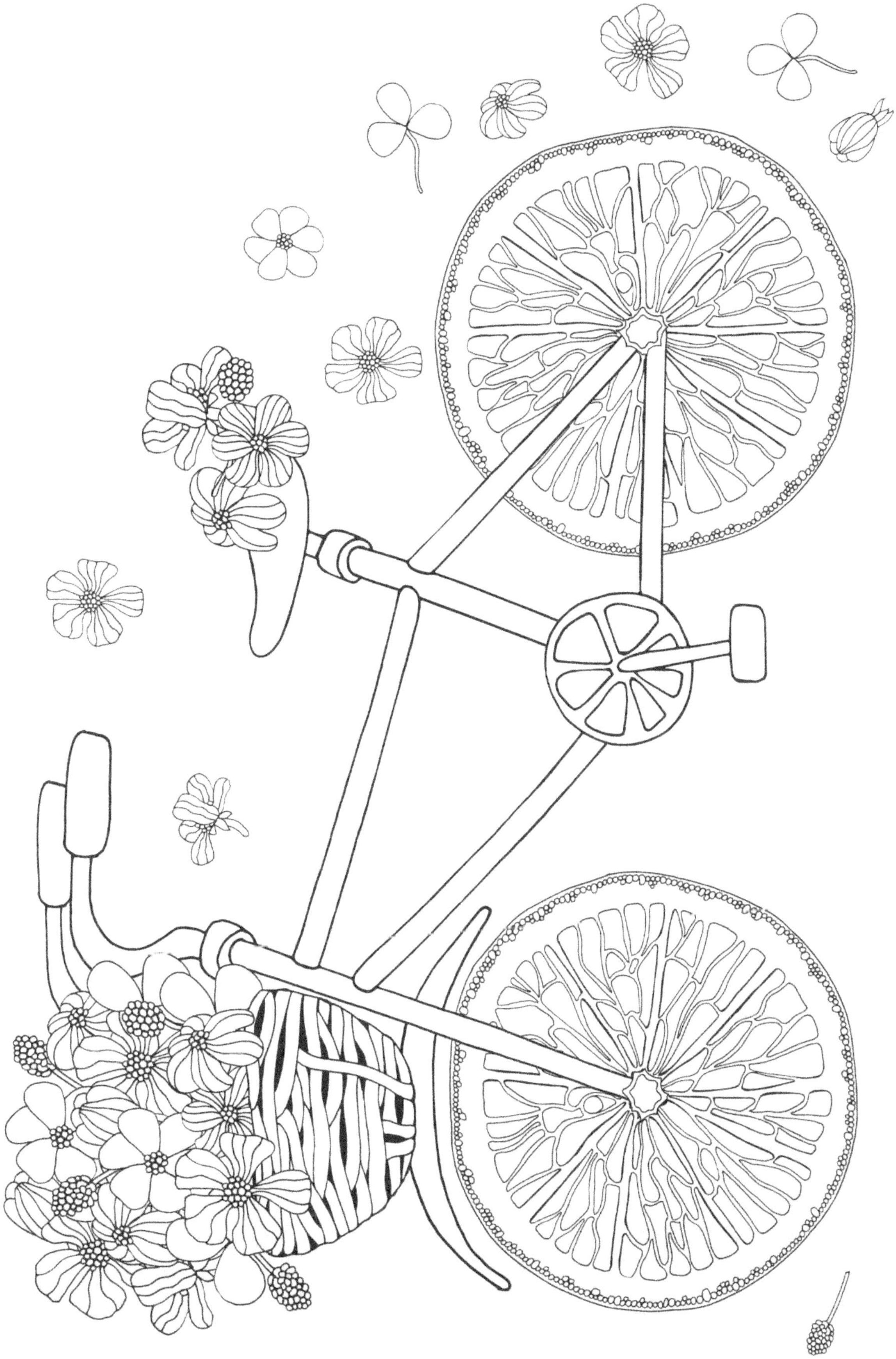

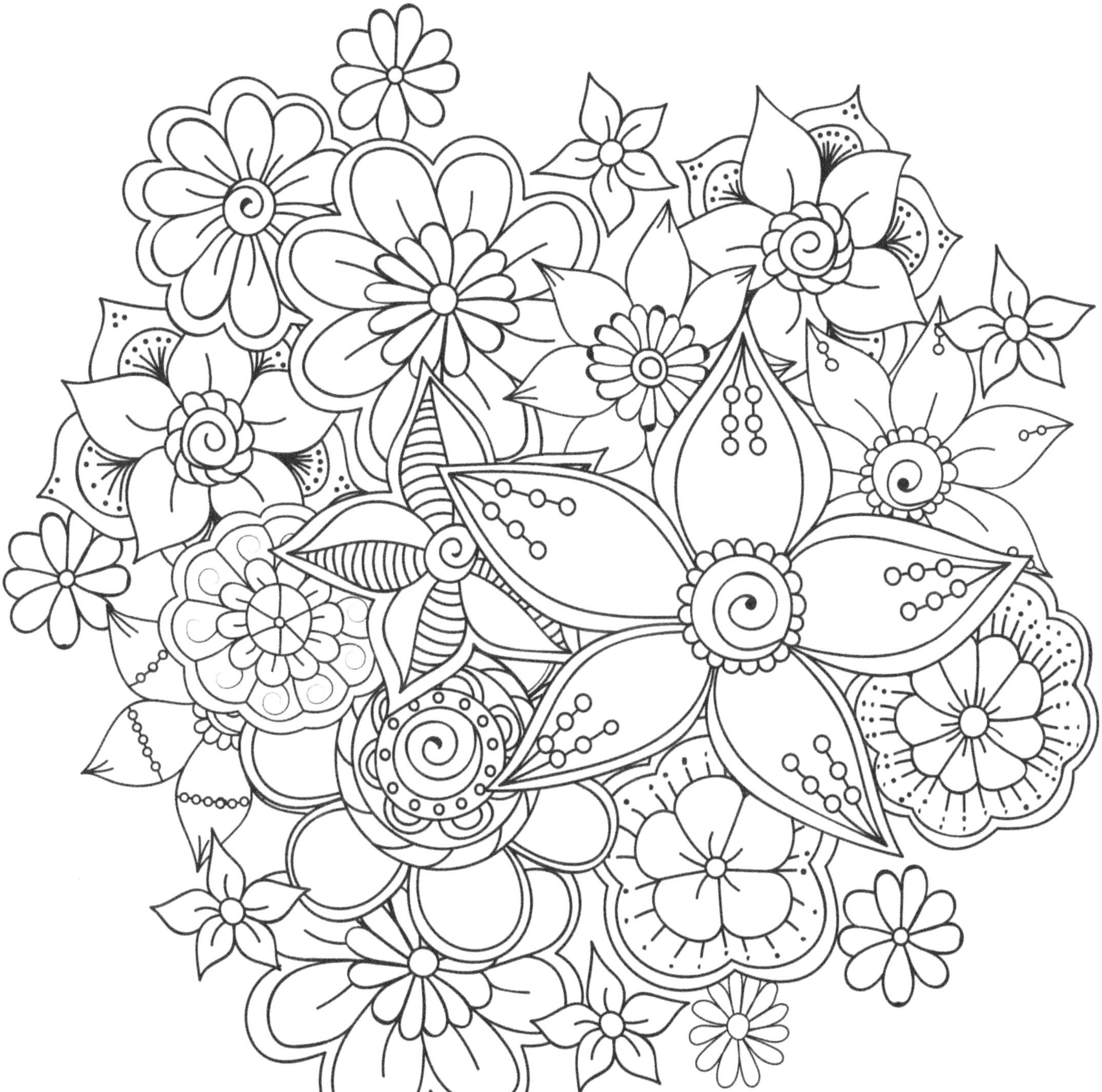

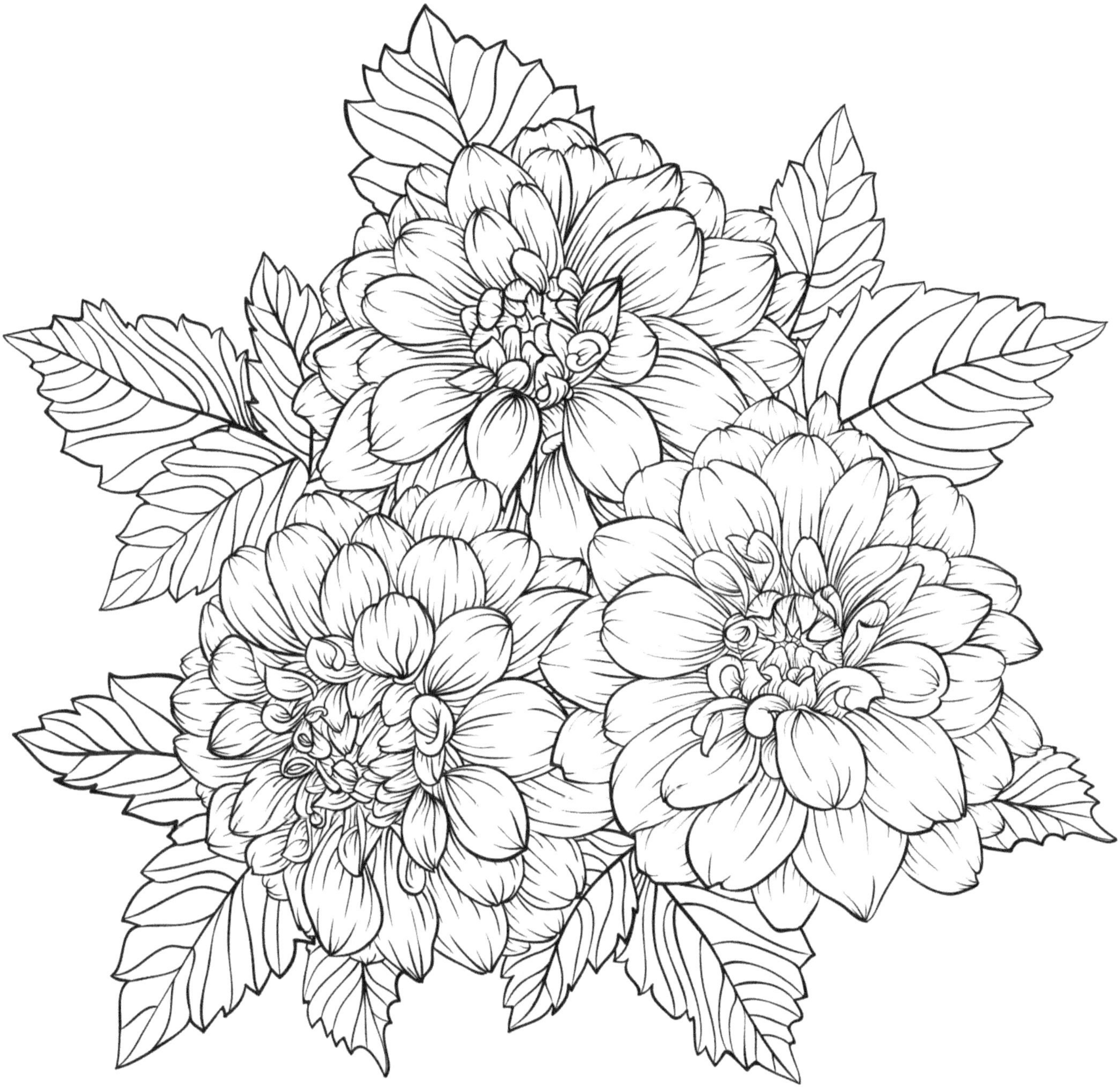

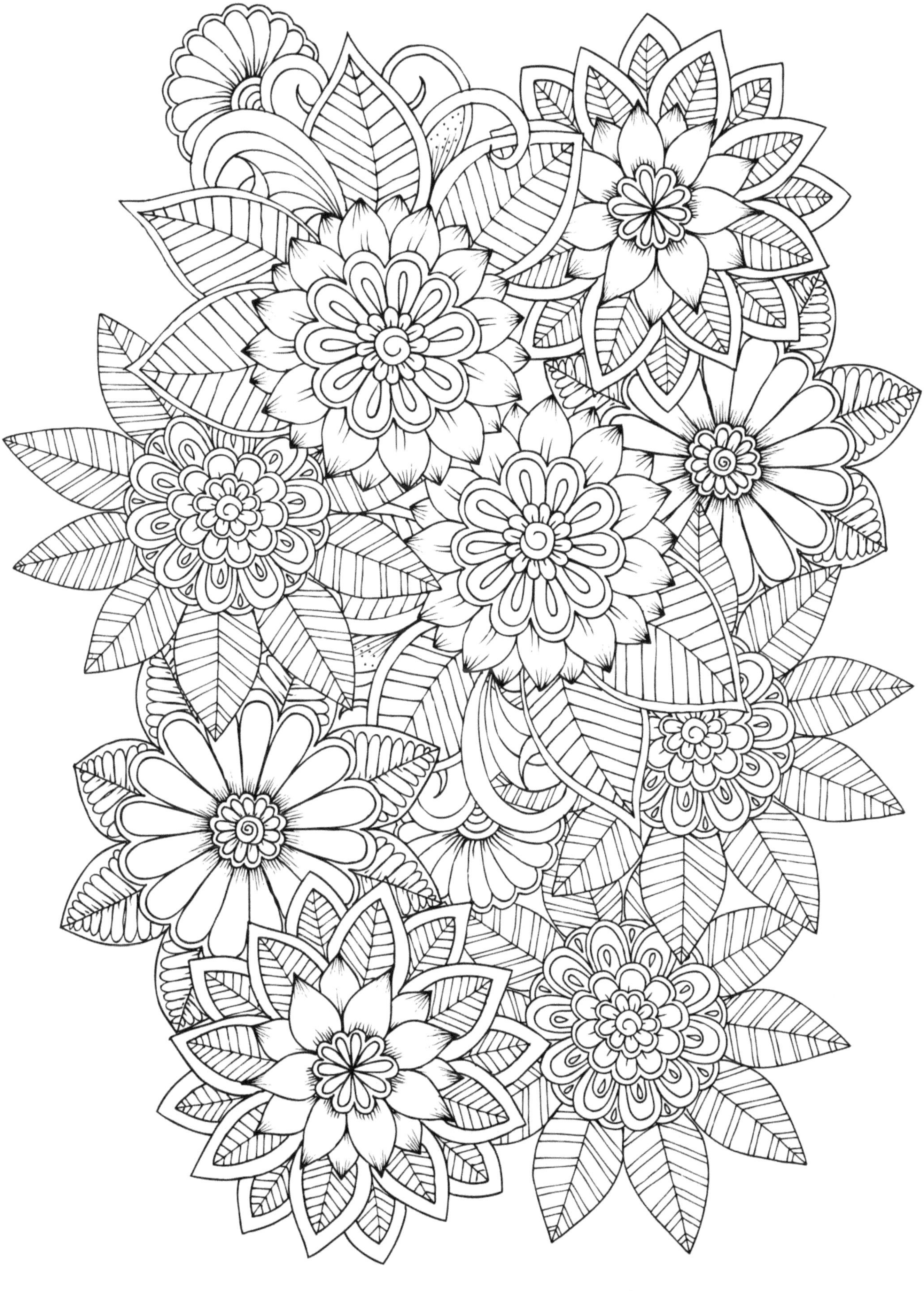